Team Building

Turn personal strengths into group success

Fifth Edition

Robert B. Maddux, Barb Wingfield, and Deborah A. Osgood

D1354859

A Crisp Fifty-Minute™ Series Book

AXZO ✦ PRESS

Team Building

Turn personal strengths into group success

Fifth Edition

Robert B. Maddux, Barb Wingfield, and Deborah A. Osgood

CREDITS:

President, Axzo Press:	**Jon Winder**
Vice President, Product Development:	**Charles G. Blum**
Vice President, Operations:	**Josh Pincus**
Director, Publishing Systems Development:	**Dan Quackenbush**
Developmental Editor:	**Brandon Heffernan**
Copy Editor:	**Catherine E. Oliver**

ISBN 10: 1-4260-1839-8
ISBN 13: 978-1-4260-1839-8
Printed in the United States of America
1 2 3 4 5 08 07 06

Table of Contents

About the Authors

This fifth edition of *Team Building* was written by Deborah Osgood, who is a U.S. Small Business Administration's Women in Business Champion, an *Enterprising Women Magazine*'s Enterprising Woman of the Year, and a recipient of the Jobs for America's Graduates Above and Beyond Leadership award. Deborah's passion for empowering individuals and teams to perform exceptionally is evidenced by numerous published training materials and countless hours serving as a career and entrepreneurial development consultant.

Deborah is founder and president of the Foundation for Entrepreneurial Research and Development (FERAD), a nonprofit organization that specializes in career empowerment, entrepreneurial research, and education. She is a consultant and advisor to government, nonprofit, and *Fortune* 500 companies in the development of interactive resource communities, curriculum, and marketing communication strategies that drive economic development and sustainability on a national scale.

Deborah holds a BBS and MBA and is a Doctoral candidate in Transformational Leadership. She welcomes your contact at Deborah.Osgood@FERAD.org, or visit www.FERAD.org.

With Sincere Thanks

The prior edition of *Team Building* was written by Barb Wingfield, the president of Green Thumb Management, author of *Reasons to Say WOW!!! A Celebration of Life's Simple Pleasures*, and co-author of *Retaining Your Employees: Using Respect, Recognition, and Rewards for Positive Results.* Barb's talent for helping people understand and improve how they interact with others contributed to the value that this Crisp book offers today.

In Memoriam

The late Robert Maddux was an extraordinary person. For more than 30 years, he designed and delivered management-skills seminars throughout the world, helping large corporations and small businesses improve their productivity. Bob also wrote several best-selling management books, including *Effective Performance Appraisals, Delegating for Results, Building Teams for Your Small Business, Job Performance and Chemical Dependency, Successful Negotiation, Quality Interviewing*, and *Ethics in Business. Team Building* was his best-selling title, and this revision is based on the concepts that Bob originally developed.

More than a million copies of Bob's books have been sold. They have served as the basis for several training videos and have been translated into more than 20 languages. Bob's genius for making complex things simple has helped untold numbers of readers worldwide become better managers. Bob was a true "people person"; his good nature and contributions to management are greatly missed, but live on through his published works.

Preface

Everything in life that is worth working for requires that we work well with and through others. This is especially true in career pursuits in which collaboration with others is often needed to achieve success. Whenever two or more people work together toward a common goal, you have the elements of a team. Because teams are made up of individuals, and individuals are by nature unique, there is no one component that will make a team successful. Instead, it's a collective process of balancing shifting interests and demands, bound together by a common purpose, that ultimately drives team success.

This book addresses the process of building and maintaining a successful team in an organizational setting. It demonstrates how planning, organizing, commitment, vision, and shared objectives contribute to performance. The foundation principles that Robert Maddux originally wrote about and that Barb Wingfield reinforced remain valid today. It's an honor to build upon their insights by bringing the content in line with today's interpersonal dynamics and organizational settings.

To assist with the understanding and implementation of these concepts, this book uses the analogy of building a house to illustrate similarities with building a team. Both processes require individuals who possess specific talents to achieve common objectives. Both processes require individual and collective coordination, and both processes depend on effective coordination to achieve successful results.

As you read each part, look for the similarities between your organizational environment and the concepts introduced. Identify which concepts make sense to you and your team, and collaborate with members to implement them. You will be delighted with the results!

Deborah A. Osgood

Acknowledgments

A book about team building would be incomplete if I failed to thank the members of my team who inspire, motivate, and encourage me to perform: my husband, Bill Osgood, whose tireless coaching and sincere encouragement got me to where I am today; my staff, whose sincere dedication and contributions keep me on my toes and provoke continued learning; the professors at Franklin Pierce University, who challenge my beliefs and spark my thirst for knowledge; the countless entrepreneurs and young adults that I have mentored, who reinforce for me that it is in giving that one truly receives; and Chris Norton, the project manager of this book, who helped to make the project fun.

Learning Objectives

Complete this book, and you'll know how to:

1) Identify the differences between a group and a team.

2) Incorporate tips for becoming an effective team leader.

3) Explore behavior styles and monitor the effect that each style has on team development.

4) Develop techniques for promoting open communication, team engagement, and productivity.

5) Benefit from facilitating both individual growth and team growth to attain shared outcomes.

Workplace and Management Competencies mapping

For over 30 years, business and industry has utilized competency models to select employees. The trend to use competency-based approaches in education and training, assessment, and development of workers has experienced a more recent emergence within the Employment and Training Administration (ETA), a division of the United States Department of Labor.

The ETA's General Competency Model Framework spans a wide array of competencies from the more basic competencies, such as reading and writing, to more advanced occupation-specific competencies. The Crisp Series finds its home in what the ETA refers to as the Workplace Competencies and the Management Competencies.

Team Building covers information vital to mastering the following competencies:

Workplace Competencies:

▶ Teamwork ▶ Creative Thinking

Management Competencies:

▶ Delegating ▶ Clarifying Roles & Objectives

▶ Supporting Others ▶ Managing Conflict & Team Building

▶ Motivating & Inspiring

For a comprehensive mapping of Crisp Series titles to the Workplace and Management competencies, visit www.CrispSeries.com.

About the Crisp 50-Minute Series

The Crisp 50-Minute Series was designed to cover critical business and professional development topics in the shortest possible time. Our easy-to-read, easy-to-understand format can be used for self-study or for classroom training. With a wealth of hands-on exercises, the 50-Minute books keep you engaged and help you retain critical skills.

What You Need to Know

We designed the Crisp 50-Minute Series to be as self-explanatory as possible. But there are a few things you should know before you begin the book.

Exercises

Exercises look like this:

EXERCISE TITLE

Questions and other information would be here.

Keep a pencil handy. Any time you see an exercise, you should try to complete it. If the exercise has specific answers, an answer key will be provided in the appendix. (Some exercises ask you to think about your own opinions or situation; these types of exercises will not have answer keys.)

Forms

A heading like this means that the rest of the page is a form:

FORMHEAD

Forms are meant to be reusable. You might want to make a photocopy of a form before you fill it out, so that you can use it again later.

A Note to Instructors

We've tried to make the Crisp 50-Minute Series books as useful as possible as classroom training manuals. Here are some of the features we provide for instructors:

- ▶ PowerPoint presentations
- ▶ Answer keys
- ▶ Assessments
- ▶ Customization

PowerPoint Presentations

You can download a PowerPoint presentation for this book from our Web site at www.CrispSeries.com.

Answer keys

If an exercise has specific answers, an answer key will be provided in the appendix. (Some exercises ask you to think about your own opinions or situation; these types of exercises will not have answer keys.)

Assessments

For each 50-Minute Series book, we have developed a 35- to 50-item assessment. The assessment for this book is available at www.CrispSeries.com. *Assessments should not be used in any employee-selection process.*

Customization

Crisp books can be quickly and easily customized to meet your needs—from adding your logo to developing proprietary content. Crisp books are available in print and electronic form. For more information on customization, see www.CrispSeries.com.

Designing a Successful Blueprint for Your Team

"*There are no problems we cannot solve together and very few that we can solve by ourselves.*"

–U.S. President Lyndon Johnson

In this part:

▶ The Purpose of a Blueprint

▶ Distinguishing Teams from Groups

▶ Group vs. Team Characteristics

▶ Group-Centered Managers vs. Team-Centered Leaders

▶ Increasing Productivity through Teamwork

▶ The Benefits of Team Building

The Purpose of a Blueprint

Before you build a house, you need a blueprint. Before you develop a blueprint, you must evaluate, select, and engage an architect or builder to discuss the features and characteristics that you want to include in the house. The blueprint is then created, serving as a guide for the builder to construct the house according to your specifications, and ensuring that the house suits your needs and tastes. The blueprint also helps the builder determine the type and quantity of materials needed and assemble the best team to achieve the desired quality and functionality.

This process is similar to the process of building a great team in your work environment. Once you identify the work objectives, you can identify the kind of team you need to assemble to achieve your objectives, just as a builder does when assembling a team of tradespeople. As with construction projects, the key to developing a great team is to take the time to first create a blueprint.

Creating a blueprint is about taking the time up front to define the qualities you require from others, as well as developing your own leadership style. This process will help you achieve greater success through teamwork.

Distinguishing Teams from Groups

People form groups for many reasons. Groups provide the basis for family living, collective safety, democratic infrastructures, recreational activities, and work. Group behavior can range from chaos to a high level of productivity, and the difference often lies in the degree to which the members of the group function as a team.

In a work environment, some managers view their staff as a group of individuals rather than as a team. As a result, overall performance is sometimes not as productive as it might be if viewed from a different perspective. The same group of people might perform better if a manager views them as a team and establishes a climate that facilitates collaboration, trust, and mutual respect.

Different Styles to Lead Each Unit

Managing a team to achieve work-related objectives requires planning and effort. Team leaders have different management styles, often shaped by the manager's life experiences, values, and formal training.

To be an effective team leader in today's dynamic organizational environment, with its rapid changes and shifting human resource needs, it's important for managers to routinely reevaluate and adjust their leadership styles. This is often the only way a manager can facilitate collaboration and foster team productivity over time.

The tables on the following pages introduce the differences between groups and teams, along with the various characteristics required to be an effective team leader. When reviewing this information, make note of any characteristics that you view as strengths or weaknesses in your own team leadership style. Over time, look for ways to adjust your style accordingly to achieve and maintain your desired business objectives and outcomes.

Group vs. Team Characteristics

To determine whether you're working with a group of individuals or a team, compare the characteristics in the two columns below. Which category would you use to describe the behaviors of your staff?

Groups	Teams
Individuals believe they are grouped together for organizational purposes only. They work independently.	Individuals recognize their interdependence and understand that individual and collective goals are best accomplished with mutual support. Time is not wasted by struggling over turf issues or striving for personal gain at others' expense.
People tend to focus on their own work objectives because they're not sufficiently involved in planning collective objectives. Their main focus is doing their job.	People take pride in their contributions and the contributions of others because they're committed to shared goals that they helped to establish.
People are told what to do, rather than being engaged in discussing what the best approach would be. New ideas are rarely encouraged.	People proactively apply their talent and knowledge and work well with others toward shared objectives and organizational success.
People distrust each other because they do not understand how their work is interrelated. There is limited opportunity for clarification and productive communication.	People participate in facilitated discussions about their work and the work of others in the context of overall organizational objectives. There is a high degree of mutual trust, and new ideas are encouraged and debated.
People are cautious about what they say, limiting their ability to focus on shared work objectives. Relationships are typically unproductive and fraught with competition, infighting, and gossip.	People are not reluctant to participate in constructive communication. Time is allocated to facilitating dialogue and supporting mutual understanding of different points of view.

(CONTINUED)

Groups	Teams
Individual training is provided to develop skills and knowledge, but there are limited opportunities to apply those skills in the actual work environment.	People are encouraged to develop new skills and knowledge and to share with others what they have learned. This shared knowledge then becomes integrated into the collective work environment.
People who find themselves in conflicts have limited options for resolving them. Group dynamics center on personality and aggression, rather than work performance and productivity.	People understand that conflicts can and will arise. However, opportunities to resolve differences quickly and constructively are provided, resulting in new ideas and innovative approaches to work.
People conclude that their viewpoints are unimportant. "Groupthink" and behavior conformity take precedence over organizational objectives and productive outcomes.	Individuals embrace organizational and collective objectives, and understand that their viewpoints and contributions have a direct effect on performance outcomes.

Group-Centered Managers vs. Team-Centered Leaders

The following table describes the differences between group-centered management and team-centered leadership. As you read through these perspectives, think about which qualities best describe your current style.

Group-Centered Management	Team-Centered Leadership
The emphasis is on getting the work done and pleasing superiors. Individual input about the work, methods, and new ideas are not relevant.	There are constant opportunities to improve work efficiencies. The people who perform the work are the best source for new ideas and innovative breakthroughs.
It's important to react to whatever upper management, peers, and employees want. The objective is to be liked by others.	Colleagues are proactively engaged in reassessing the status quo. Collaboration and mutual respect are encouraged.
Individuals sometimes have good ideas, but they are not reliable. It is up to the manager to do the planning and problem solving.	People are empowered to get involved and to be committed to achieving individual and collective goals. Growth opportunities are routinely provided.
Individuals who suggest that they know more than their boss are not to be trusted.	Performance, productivity, and profitability are driven by securing and continually motivating individuals who are the best in their fields.
Individuals need to figure out how to solve their own problems. That's why they get paid.	Because of continually competing demands for time and resources, assisting with problem solving is an important part of a manager's job.
Individuals lack the capacity to understand the big picture. That's why the manager makes the big bucks.	Supporting open communication helps to ensure that everyone is working together toward shared outcomes.
Conflicts between staff members or other groups are not my problem.	Mediating conflict before it becomes destructive is necessary to ensure success.

(CONTINUED)

Group-Centered Management	Team-Centered Leadership
Recognizing individual achievements is part of the annual performance review process.	Routinely acknowledging and building upon individual and collective achievements helps to build a stronger foundation for collaboration.
Fear can often be an effective motivator for getting the work done on time and under budget.	Mutual trust and respect are important parts of supporting the success of any organization.

"This morning we'll do some head-butting,
then this afternoon we'll break out into team training."

Increasing Productivity Through Teamwork

There are many types of groups, with varied purposes and goals. Whether groups are organized to function within business, community, or governmental arenas, all groups can achieve more when they work as teams.

When productive teams are compared with less productive groups, important differences are revealed. Here is an example: A study was conducted of several retailers operating within the same industry, drawing from the same labor pool, and subject to the same licensing requirements. Profitability was measured in terms of revenue per square foot.

One retailer dramatically outperformed industry rivals. It had an average growth rate of 11 percent per year, almost triple the industry average, and its revenues per square foot were twice as high as that of its traditional competitors.

This study concluded that the differences between retailer performance and outcomes were due to the way management worked with employees. The most profitable retailer provided employees with significantly more individual responsibility and involvement in goal setting, problem solving, and sharing of rewards based on outcomes.

Teamwork Throughout the Organization

Effective teamwork is possible and relevant throughout any organization. It's just as important among senior executives, who establish the organizational mission and vision, as it is among the managers and employees, who contribute their skills and talents in implementing these strategies. The absence of teamwork in any organization (or between functional areas) will limit productivity and growth, and might ultimately result in going out of business.

Building a productive team is possible at any time and under virtually any circumstances. You need to facilitate collaboration and foster trust and mutual respect among participants—people who share a common mission and vision. Being proactive and working to develop and maintain solid team-leading skills over time will contribute significantly to your attaining the desired results.

Within effective teams, individuals feel a sense of belonging. Each participant understands his or her role and how it fits into the bigger picture, and is willing to contribute his or her talents to attain shared outcomes. In the context of the house-building example discussed previously, few individuals possess the complete set of skills required to construct the foundation, engineer the electrical infrastructure, and install the plumbing systems. Under the guidance of an effective team leader, however, each tradesperson understands what needs to done—how, when, and where to contribute his or her talents to create a high-quality product.

When participants understand their individual and collective purpose and willingly work together, they are transformed from a group into a team. When participants are unsure about the purpose of their role and how it relates to others, they typically work as individuals to protect themselves and their job security. This situation can significantly compromise overall performance and satisfaction among all participants. The key to success as a team leader is a willingness to plan for success, engage others in the process, and monitor and make adjustments over time.

> *When teamwork works well, you feel a deep level of connection to team members. The energy you receive from the experience builds an unstoppable momentum that makes you feel that anything is possible and achievable."*
>
> **–Christine Zust**

The Benefits of Team Building

Many managers underestimate the value of team building. Most success stories are, in one way or another, the result of working well with others. Investing the time to build effective leadership skills as a manager requires continuous effort, but results in continuous rewards.

HOW SUCCESSFUL IS YOUR TEAM-BUILDING?

Review the following list and check (✔) which rewards you are currently realizing, or would like to realize, among your team.

_____ 1. Work objectives are routinely achieved on time and within budget because they are established as a result of individual and collective input among team members.

_____ 2. There is mutual trust and respect between all members of the team.

_____ 3. Communication is open. Dialogue regarding new ideas, innovative approaches to tasks, and goal setting is encouraged and supported.

_____ 4. Problem solving is effective because the team's expertise is leveraged.

_____ 5. Performance is consistent and high because team members establish and understand individual and collective performance standards and celebrate shared outcomes.

_____ 6. Conflict is replaced by valuing and respecting individual differences and viewpoints, thereby creating opportunities to approach work differently through facilitated discussion and open communication.

_____ 7. There is a constructive balance between performance expectations for the overall team and for individual participants.

_____ 8. The team is recognized for outstanding results, and individuals are recognized for their respective contributions.

CONTINUED

CONTINUED

_____ 9. Encouraging the expression and testing of new ideas stimulates creativity and drives performance.

_____ 10. Individuals understand that succeeding as a team takes precedence over achieving individual success at the expense of others.

_____ 11. Developing effective team leadership skills provides an opportunity in which all participants add value and all receive value; the organization benefits from improved productivity; the team benefits through recognition; and individuals benefit through career advancement opportunities.

> *Everything in life is about working well with and through others. Strong teams get positive results.*"
>
> **–Deborah Osgood**

When team building is understood and applied throughout the organization, transforming groups into teams becomes much easier. Willingness and a positive attitude toward team building are essential components of this process.

DOES YOUR ATTITUDE SUPPORT TEAM BUILDING?

For each statement below, circle the number that best describes your attitude: 7 means that you agree with the statement; and 1 means that you don't. When you have finished, add up the circled numbers and write the total in the space provided.

1. I select employees based on job qualifications and an ability to work well with others.   7 6 5 4 3 2 1

2. I empower employees to do their best by involving them in goal setting, problem solving, and productivity improvement.   7 6 5 4 3 2 1

3. I facilitate collaboration by providing a basis by which individuals can effectively work together.   7 6 5 4 3 2 1

4. I lead through example, communicating with people openly and honestly while encouraging the same in return.   7 6 5 4 3 2 1

5. I keep agreements with my team members because their trust is essential to my leadership.   7 6 5 4 3 2 1

6. I arrange meetings and other venues to assist team members in building mutual trust and respect and in valuing individual talents and abilities.   7 6 5 4 3 2 1

7. I work with individuals to ensure access to training and opportunities to apply what they learn.   7 6 5 4 3 2 1

8. I transform conflicts into opportunities for further learning and personal growth.   7 6 5 4 3 2 1

9. I believe that people welcome the opportunity to perform as a team when expectations are clear and rewards are fair.   7 6 5 4 3 2 1

10. I am willing to accept the situation when an individual chooses not to work on a team, and I help the person find a more suitable position.   7 6 5 4 3 2 1

TOTAL: _____

CONTINUED

CONTINUED

If your total score in this exercise was:

60–70   You have a positive attitude about managing people in a way that fosters collaboration and leads to building and maintaining an effective team environment.

40–59   Consider reevaluating your management style, and look for ways to further develop your leadership skills.

Below 40   Consider adopting some of the team-building principles introduced in this book or seeking additional training. Even a small shift in attitude can bring about profound improvements in performance.

Team-Building Tip: *Approach people with respect. Approach tasks with a can-do attitude.*

CASE STUDY: Can This Manager Be Saved?

Three months ago, Chris was promoted to a position that requires managing five people. This is the first time that she has been responsible for the work of others in addition to her own work, and she has received little training.

Although each employee has a different job description with distinct functions, the work is interrelated and overall success is highly dependent on a cooperative effort between employees. Chris has worked hard to establish expectations, assign tasks, and communicate deadlines. However, two employees are consistently having trouble meeting deadlines, and constant bickering among the group is further contributing to delays and frustrations for everyone.

Chris realizes that she has to do something, but she is already overwhelmed with her own work and reporting requirements. As the hostility mounts and productivity continues to fall below expectations, she finds herself spending more and more time working, yet getting fewer results. Her fear of getting fired is growing stronger every day.

What are some things that Chris can do to overcome her fear and turn around the performance of her group?

_____

_____

_____

_____

_____

_____

_____

_____

Compare your answer with the authors' responses in the Appendix.

Part Summary

Managing a team to achieve work-related objectives requires planning and effort. Take time up front to create a blueprint for your team by defining the qualities you require from others and developing your own leadership style.

Building a productive team is possible at any time and under virtually any circumstances. Facilitate collaboration and foster trust and mutual respect among participants who share a common mission and vision. Be proactive and work to develop and maintain solid team-leading skills, and you will be more likely to achieve your desired results.

P A R T 2

Building a Strong

Foundation

The loftier the building, the deeper must the foundation be laid."

–Thomas Kempis

In this part:

- ▶ The Importance of a Strong Foundation
- ▶ Taking the Time to Plan
- ▶ Applying Organizational Skills
- ▶ Building a Climate for Motivation
- ▶ Establishing Accountability

The Importance of a Strong Foundation

A strong foundation is essential if you want to build a sturdy house that will stand the test of time. The foundation supports all aspects of the house and determines the overall structural integrity. If the foundation is poor, the structure will gradually shift over time, resulting in cracks in walls and broken pipes.

A successful team must also be built upon a foundation that provides strength and integrity. Like the functional performance of a house, team performance is also interrelated. If your team is weak in one area, you risk poor performance in that area and other areas over time. To avoid or minimize such outcomes, you need to plan ahead and build a strong team foundation.

To build a proper house foundation, you must have a valid blueprint, sufficient resources, and a specific outcome in mind. The same is true when building a team foundation. You must understand what the team's purpose is, what skill sets and other resources are needed to fulfill that purpose, and what success will look like when you attain it.

This part is about the process of developing a strong team foundation. Through planning, organizing, motivating, and establishing accountability systems, you will learn how to create a highly productive team.

Taking the Time to Plan

The better that people understand what is expected of them, the more effective they will be in meeting expectations. Without clarity about why the team exists, what the shared objectives are, and what resources are available to achieve team objectives, frustration is likely to set in. Frustration usually stems from confusion, and confusion is often the result of poor planning.

Failing to plan is planning to fail. As the leader of the team, you must take the time to plan. It's critical to building a strong team foundation.

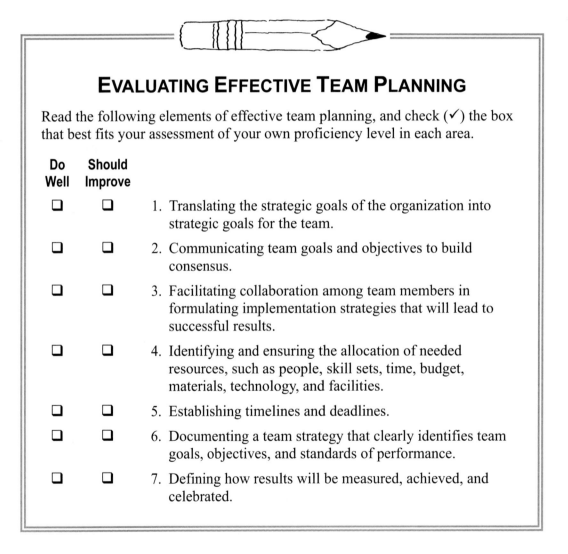

EVALUATING EFFECTIVE TEAM PLANNING

Read the following elements of effective team planning, and check (✓) the box that best fits your assessment of your own proficiency level in each area.

Do Well	Should Improve	
❏	❏	1. Translating the strategic goals of the organization into strategic goals for the team.
❏	❏	2. Communicating team goals and objectives to build consensus.
❏	❏	3. Facilitating collaboration among team members in formulating implementation strategies that will lead to successful results.
❏	❏	4. Identifying and ensuring the allocation of needed resources, such as people, skill sets, time, budget, materials, technology, and facilities.
❏	❏	5. Establishing timelines and deadlines.
❏	❏	6. Documenting a team strategy that clearly identifies team goals, objectives, and standards of performance.
❏	❏	7. Defining how results will be measured, achieved, and celebrated.

Team-Building Tip: *Engaging your team early on in the planning process fosters collaboration, encourages individual ownership, and leverages diverse skill sets. Effective leadership is about effective facilitation.*

Applying Organizational Skills

With a solid plan in place, the next step is to get organized. Being organized supports operational efficiency, and efficiency supports productivity. When teams are operating efficiently and productively, they are contributing to increased capacity. In turn, increased operational capacity contributes to profitability. And when the company is profitable, everyone benefits.

To get to the profitable stage, you must organize three key assets when building a team: people, processes, and technology. Organizing people involves understanding who is on your team, what their skills sets are, and how to motivate them. You need to organize the resources required to coordinate the delivery of services and/or the production of products. Organizing technology requires taking full advantage of innovations that offer quality assurance, operational efficiencies, and competitive advantages.

EVALUATING ORGANIZATIONAL SKILLS

Read the following aspects of effective organizational skills, and check (✔) the box that best fits your assessment of your own proficiency level in each area.

Do Well	Should Improve	
❑	❑	1. Translating complex strategies into manageable and realistic tasks.
❑	❑	2. Utilizing people, processes, and technology to achieve goals.
❑	❑	3. Aggregating resources, delegating tasks, and assigning responsibilities based on team members' needs and skill sets.
❑	❑	4. Facilitating collaboration among team members and between other parties to support process efficiencies and drive results.
❑	❑	5. Leveraging technology to drive performance quality, efficiency, and competitive advantage.
❑	❑	6. Establishing and maintaining communication channels that support information sharing, feedback, and collective progress.

Building a Climate for Motivation

Successful managers understand that individual team members are responsible for their own motivation. What the manager is responsible for is fostering an atmosphere where everyone feels recognized and valued for who they are and what they offer the team.

Building a productive and motivating climate is similar to creating a productive climate for a garden. High-quality nutrients in the soil and plenty of water and sunshine will help seeds grow, ultimately producing a lush garden. A high-quality plan, sufficient resources, and plenty of recognition will help motivate people to work well, individually and collectively, toward shared outcomes.

Open Communication

A motivating climate in the workplace requires open communication. Most people want to know what is expected of them and where they stand in the eyes of their employer or manager. They want to feel comfortable asking questions and introducing new ideas, and they want to feel as though their ideas are valued. The more comfortable they feel, the more motivated they are to perform.

There are many approaches to maintaining open communication. With an open-door policy, managers encourage employees to stop by their offices with questions and suggestions. Sometimes managers visit individual employee workstations to proactively facilitate such communication. Team meetings also provide opportunities for open communication.

Whatever the technique, the point is to be sensitive to the needs of team members to ensure open lines of communication. Doing so will foster a climate in which people are more motivated to work toward achieving organizational objectives.

Individual Motivations

Motivation about work varies from person to person. Some people choose a position because of where they live, while others choose where to live because they want a particular position. It's important for a team leader to understand what motivates an individual, as well as what motivates a team. With a productive balance between the two, individual needs can be satisfied and organizational objectives attained.

Because motivation is personal, developing a productive balance between individual and collective interests will require time and effort. The results are worth it, as the following case study illustrates.

CASE STUDY: Recognizing Individual and Collective Contributions

Mike was recently recruited to fill the position of Vice President of Information Systems. Upon starting his new job, he learned that his team was several days behind schedule and at risk of going significantly over budget to finish a job for an important new client.

Not wanting to begin his new career opportunity on such a negative note, he made an appointment with the Human Resources manager to inquire about policies regarding employee incentives. Much to his surprise, no formal policies were in place. After asking a few more questions, Mike learned that the company did provide other forms of employee benefits, including free tickets to sporting events; discounts at area retailers, including a travel agency and a fitness center; and free membership at a wholesale distribution warehouse.

After this meeting, Mike called his team together for a brainstorming session, in which he facilitated individual input and encouraged new ideas about how the work might be done more efficiently and what it might take to get back on schedule. During the meeting, he received many good ideas, and he learned that his predecessor never held similar types of team meetings.

Next, Mike met with his boss and proposed the following: "Jane, my team is several days behind schedule and at risk of going over budget by 26% on the project with our new client. I've met with the team and they believe that they can get things back on schedule. When they do, I'd like your permission to spend 2% of my team's weekly payroll budget to reward them for their efforts."

Jane agreed, the team pulled together, the project was finished on time and within budget, and the client was thrilled. Mike divided up the reward budget, giving each member of his team a gift card that could be used to purchase merchandise at a number of local retailers.

Thanks to Mike's creative and innovative approach to team building, the company learned a valuable lesson about building a climate for motivation, facilitating open communication, and rewarding individual and collective efforts for a job well done.

HOW WELL DO YOU MOTIVATE OTHERS?

Read the following motivational factors, and check (✓) the box that best fits your assessment of your own proficiency level in each area. Collectively, these elements work to support the success of individuals and teams.

Do Well	Should Improve	
❏	❏	1. Ensuring that each employee knows what is expected, how performance will be measured, and how success will be rewarded.
❏	❏	2. Facilitating open communication by getting to know employees as individuals and understanding what motivates them.
❏	❏	3. Mutually establishing individual and collective team objectives, and making training available to support outcomes.
❏	❏	4. Listening, and ensuring access to required resources that support performance.
❏	❏	5. Fostering an environment of collaboration and mutual respect, while guiding and encouraging professional growth.
❏	❏	6. Recognizing and rewarding good performance, and correcting or eliminating poor performance.

Team-Building Tip: *Effective leaders work to build a climate of motivation, in which open communication is facilitated and team members are recognized for their individual and collective contributions.*

Establishing Accountability

Few things in life remain constant. As a plan is launched, as resources are organized, and as motivated team members interact, change occurs. Because of this, a team leader must continually monitor progress against objectives. Through a process for maintaining accountability, a leader will have in place a system of checks and balances that will reveal when things are veering off course.

Accountability requires assigning objectives to specific team members during the initial planning process. Once the plan is launched, there are assigned checkpoints for connecting with team members to assess progress and compare it to goals. When there are discrepancies, strategies must be developed to restore balance and ultimately achieve established outcomes. It's important for team members to accept responsibility for agreed-upon outcomes in this process.

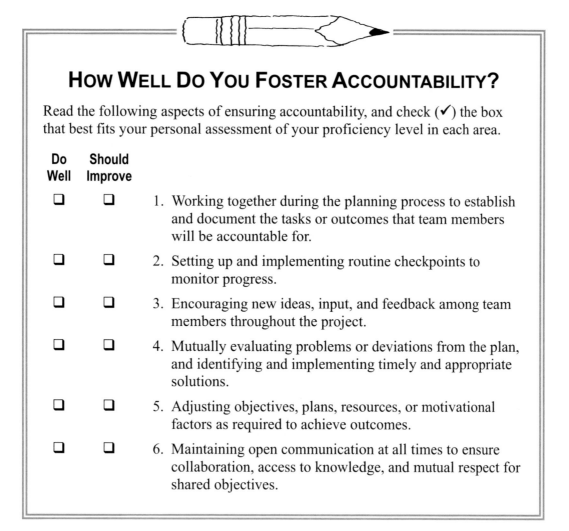

HOW WELL DO YOU FOSTER ACCOUNTABILITY?

Read the following aspects of ensuring accountability, and check (✓) the box that best fits your personal assessment of your proficiency level in each area.

Do Well	Should Improve	
❑	❑	1. Working together during the planning process to establish and document the tasks or outcomes that team members will be accountable for.
❑	❑	2. Setting up and implementing routine checkpoints to monitor progress.
❑	❑	3. Encouraging new ideas, input, and feedback among team members throughout the project.
❑	❑	4. Mutually evaluating problems or deviations from the plan, and identifying and implementing timely and appropriate solutions.
❑	❑	5. Adjusting objectives, plans, resources, or motivational factors as required to achieve outcomes.
❑	❑	6. Maintaining open communication at all times to ensure collaboration, access to knowledge, and mutual respect for shared objectives.

Team-Building Tip: *Individual ability and the willingness to accept responsibility are key components of ensuring accountability and performance.*

CASE STUDY: Which Leadership Style Would You Prefer?

Morgan and Aidan have both been promoted to their first management positions. Both had considerable experience as senior technicians before the promotions. One day during lunch, Morgan and Aidan exchanged their ideas about how they planned to make the transition from technician to manager.

Morgan volunteered that she plans to concentrate on defining the work that needs to be done and providing her employees with precise goals and performance standards regarding her expectations. Because of her direct experience and knowledge, she will also prepare a detailed plan of accountability for each employee. She believes that this approach will ensure that goals are met while giving her total control over outcomes.

Aidan responded by stating that he had already secured his manager's approval to participate in a management training program. In the meantime, he also intends to engage the members of his team in day-to-day planning, organizing, and problem solving. Aiden is confident that he can learn to become an effective leader, and he believes that every member of his team is competent and can make important contributions to overall effectiveness. He also believes that people welcome the satisfaction that comes from being involved in establishing project objectives and outcomes.

Which of these managers would you prefer to work with, and why?

_____

_____

_____

_____

_____

Compare your answer with the authors' responses in the Appendix

Part Summary

A successful team must be built on a foundation that provides strength and integrity. If your team is weak in one area, you risk poor performance in that area and in other areas over time. To avoid or minimize poor outcomes, you need to plan ahead and build a strong team foundation. As the team leader, you must take the time to plan. It's critical to building a strong team foundation.

With a solid plan in place, the next steps are to get organized and create a motivating climate. You need to foster an atmosphere in which everyone feels recognized and valued for who they are and what they offer the team. A motivating climate requires open communication. Most people want to know what is expected of them and where they stand in the eyes of their employer or manager.

To ensure accountability among team members, an effective team leader must assign objectives to specific team members during the planning process. Once the plan is launched, establish checkpoints for connecting with team members to mutually assess progress against goals. When there are discrepancies, develop strategies to restore balance and achieve the desired outcomes.

Team-Building Tip: *Leverage employee knowledge and experience when organizing resources. Innovation and creativity can be powerful team assets.*

"We were just here for a brainstorming meeting.
Please say you did not throw away the napkins."

Constructing a

Solid Framework

"*To find out what one is fitted to do, and to secure an opportunity to do it, is the key to happiness.*"

—John Dewey

In this part:

- ▶ Assembling Your Team
- ▶ Combining Diverse Behavior Styles
  - ▷ The Promoting Style
  - ▷ The Directive Style
  - ▷ The Analytical Style
  - ▷ The Supportive Style
- ▶ Leveraging the Strengths of Each Style
- ▶ Building a Solid Team Through Training
- ▶ Promoting Teamwork Through Your Leadership Style

Assembling Your Team

Once you have developed your blueprint and built your foundation, you're ready to begin assembling your team. It's important to understand what components make up a productive team and how to put one together.

People are the most critical part of an organization's success. Achieving team goals requires qualified, motivated people. As a team leader, your role is to select the right people, facilitate their work, and guide them in working well with each other.

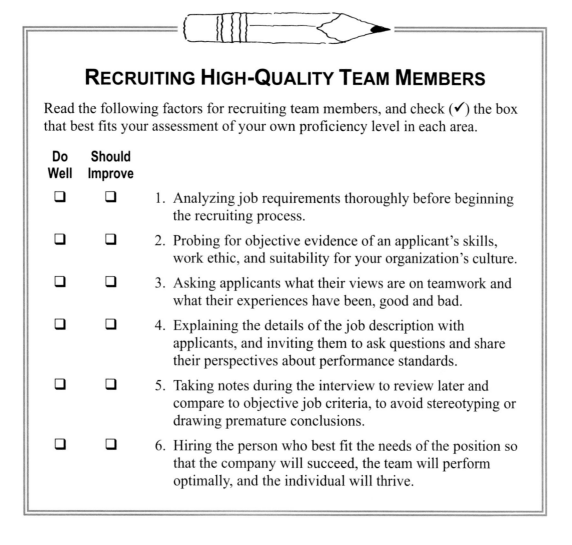

RECRUITING HIGH-QUALITY TEAM MEMBERS

Read the following factors for recruiting team members, and check (✓) the box that best fits your assessment of your own proficiency level in each area.

Do Well	Should Improve	
❏	❏	1. Analyzing job requirements thoroughly before beginning the recruiting process.
❏	❏	2. Probing for objective evidence of an applicant's skills, work ethic, and suitability for your organization's culture.
❏	❏	3. Asking applicants what their views are on teamwork and what their experiences have been, good and bad.
❏	❏	4. Explaining the details of the job description with applicants, and inviting them to ask questions and share their perspectives about performance standards.
❏	❏	5. Taking notes during the interview to review later and compare to objective job criteria, to avoid stereotyping or drawing premature conclusions.
❏	❏	6. Hiring the person who best fit the needs of the position so that the company will succeed, the team will perform optimally, and the individual will thrive.

Team-Building Tip: *If the people you choose for your team are not successful, you will not be successful. If you need to improve your selection and placement practices, do it now.*

Combining Diverse Behavior Styles

Assembling a team involves assembling different people and asking them to work well together. Because people have different personalities, you will also be combining diverse behavioral styles. Diversity in a team is a powerful asset. Individual backgrounds, experiences, knowledge, and skill sets each contribute to how a person behaves and each person offers something of value to the team.

When you're recruiting team members, it helps to understand the personalities involved so that you can build a team that will collaborate effectively to achieve organizational objectives. Behavioral styles can be assessed in many ways, and there are a variety of tools to help managers with this process. Commonly called *personality assessments*, these tools offer valuable insights into a person's primary and supporting behavioral characteristics.

Although such assessment tools can be valuable, it's not always necessary to use them to identify a person's tendency to behave in certain ways. When you learn what to look for and listen for, you can determine, with a high degree of accuracy, how a person is likely to behave, given a variety of team situations and work scenarios.

In her book *The Business of Listening*[1], author Diana Bonet introduces four behavioral styles that are common to most people. Each of us tends to fit one of the four styles as our primary mode of behavior, with the other three being supportive styles that are not dominant aspects. Understanding these behavior styles will help you to develop a productive team. The four styles are:

▶ Promoting

▶ Directive

▶ Analytical

▶ Supportive

Each person's dominant behavioral style provides important personality clues, including one's natural communication style. The pages that follow outline the main characteristics of each style.

---

[1]For more information on behavior or personality styles, read the Crisp Series books *The Business of Listening*, by Diana Bonet, and *Accountability*, by Sam R. Lloyd.

The Promoting Style

The Upside: People who fit into the promoting style of behavior have a lot of energy. Their positive, outgoing nature is infectious and often helps to motivate others. Promoters can see the "big picture." They are inventive, confident, and idealistic about reaching goals. In meetings, they help to keep things stirred up through humor and by injecting ideas (even when they are not asked for). Promoters are sociable and generally fun to be around.

The Downside: Although promoters offer innovative and creative ideas, they tend to lack the ability or interest to follow through on their ideas. They prefer to leave the details to someone else. Because of their constantly positive nature, they also tend to over-promise, which can lead to disappointment. These tendencies can make promoters appear somewhat superficial and disorganized, but when properly managed, they can provide the spark needed to motivate a team.

EXPLORING THE PROMOTING STYLE

Do you think this is your style?   ❑ Yes   ❑ No

Name someone famous whom you view as being a promoter.

_____

Is there a promoter on your team or in your work environment?

_____

Is there a promoter you know in your personal life?

_____

What can a promoter bring to your team?

_____

How might the downside characteristics of a promoter affect your team?

_____

What steps might you want to take to avoid these possible disadvantages?

_____

The Directive Style

The Upside: A directive style of behavior can be likened to a human bulldozer. When something needs to be done, you can count on this behavioral style to overcome obstacles, dismiss excuses, and deliver results. This focused, take-charge style approaches problems realistically and boldly.

As part of a team, a director will dominate and control others assertively, with a total commitment to winning. People with the directive style tend to be realists who recognize that both time and money are scarce resources, not to be wasted. When the going gets tough, they are the tough ones that get going. Directors also expect comparable rewards for their dedication, reliability, and achievements.

The Downside: Directors are not typically humble. Because winning is such a primary motivator, and they are good at it, they tend to have considerable egos that seek constant gratification. They're often more interested in being understood than in understanding others, and as a result, they might not always share credit when results are team driven. Although these behavioral tendencies can make them insensitive and poor listeners, directors can be a secret weapon when deadlines are near, resources are tight, and results are still expected.

EXPLORING THE DIRECTIVE STYLE

Do you think this is your style?   ❑ Yes   ❑ No

Name someone famous who you think is a director.

_____

Is there a director on your team or in your work environment?

_____

Is there a director you know in your personal life?

_____

What can a director bring to your team?

_____

How might the downside characteristics of a director affect your team?

_____

What steps might you want to take to avoid these possible disadvantages?

_____

The Analytical Style

The Upside: The analytical style of behavior is all about being logical. Analytical people tend to be well organized, neat, and precise. As a result, they will often choose professions in which these qualities are valued and well suited, such as engineering, science, accounting, programming, and research. Excellent problem solvers, these people contribute to the performance of a team by paying attention to details, thoroughly analyzing options, and proposing practical and tactical strategies. With patience and calm, they can often be relied upon to keep agreements and contribute to achieving deadlines.

The Downside: While analytical personalities offer detail-oriented commitment and focus, these qualities can also manifest as self-importance. Their emphasis on details and accuracy can also slow down performance, as the desire to be perfect often supersedes a respect for deadlines. With balance, however, this behavioral style can be a valuable team asset when objectives require precision and quality control.

EXPLORING THE ANALYTICAL STYLE

Do you think this is your style?   ❏ Yes   ❏ No

Name someone famous whom you view as being analytical.

_____

Is there an analytical person on your team or in your work environment?

_____

Is there an analytical person you know in your personal life?

_____

How can you use the strengths of an analytical person to help your team?

_____

How might the downside characteristics of an analytical person affect your team?

_____

What steps might you want to take to avoid these possible disadvantages?

_____

The Supportive Style

The Upside: Someone with a supportive personality style is friendly and eager to help others, so they are important members of the team. They are easygoing and upbeat, and they have a tendency to "go with the flow." With such a collaborative nature, they often prefer to work in groups and make decisions by consensus. When making decisions, they take into account how potential outcomes will affect other people. They tend to be peacemakers, preferring group harmony over conflict.

The Downside: While supportive personalities are great to have around as peacekeepers, their desire for acceptance can make them say and do things that are different from what they really think. They can be easy targets for others who might exploit them by asking for favors, which they know will be granted because supportive personalities often prefer the social interaction and the opportunity to please, instead of getting their own work done. Supportive personalities might fail to meet deadlines because of over-extending themselves with extraneous duties, but they can also be the glue that keeps a team together.

EXPLORING THE SUPPORTING STYLE

Do you think this is your style?   ❑ Yes   ❑ No

Name someone famous whom you view as being supportive.

_____

Is there a supportive person on your team or in your work environment?

_____

Is there a supportive person you know in your personal life?

_____

How can you use the strengths of a supportive person to help your team?

_____

How might the downside characteristics of a supportive person affect your team?

_____

What steps might you want to take to avoid these possible disadvantages?

_____

Leveraging the Strengths of Each Style

Although each personality style offers advantages and disadvantages, the objective of the team leader is to leverage the upside of each personality style when managing outcomes. Human interaction is often referred to as "chemistry"—the right mix of elements (people) often leads to successful outcomes. The key is to know what ingredients you have, and how they behave and interact, and then combine them accordingly to achieve the desired results.

For example, when a team is about to complete a project ahead of schedule and under budget, it might be appropriate to plan a celebration. In this situation, a team leader might want to engage the promoter to develop an idea, which the analytical person will then turn into a plan of action. Getting the supportive team member involved can help to get everyone interested and motivated toward achieving objectives. The directive personality can be offered the role of making a speech at the celebration to acknowledge the team's success.

LEVERAGING YOUR BEHAVIORAL STYLE

Which of the four behavioral styles most closely matches your personality?

_____

What do you think is the best quality that you bring to your team?

_____

How can the team best use your strengths to achieve team goals?

_____

_____

Is the team using your strengths to the fullest?   ❑ Yes   ❑ No

If your answer is no, how could you work to better use your strengths?

_____

_____

_____

Building a Solid Team Through Training

In today's dynamic, fast-paced world, change is unavoidable and constant. A business plan used to serve as a five-year strategy, but plans are now written for one or two years and are updated every six months. For any organization today, this means that employees' skills must be frequently and efficiently refined through training if the organization is to remain competitive and profitable.

Classroom Training

Classroom training can be a valuable approach to employee training, and it can be a productive venue for facilitating collaboration, trust, and team building because people are physically together. When job performance requires exceptional human interaction skills, such as in sales, customer service, and marketing, classroom training is often an ideal venue.

On-the-Job Training

On-the-job training involves developing employees' skills within the actual work environment so that people can apply what they are learning to real work situations.

Like classroom training, on-the-job training benefits from a well-structured approach, in which both the trainer and the trainee understand the learning objectives, their respective roles, how the learning will occur, and how outcomes will be measured. This approach typically involves a well-established training program that includes a trainer guide, a trainee guide, and related learning aids to ensure consistency in results.

Technology-Based Training

Thanks to myriad advancements in technology, there are many ways to train employees on virtually any topic by using computers, the Internet, DVDs, CD-ROMs, portable operating devices (PODs), videos, Webinars, podcasts, and social media venues. Innovations such as translation software, high-speed audio and video transmission capacities, and holographic projections also permit access to training from virtually anywhere in the world, at any time.

Advancements in these areas permit *just-in-time* (JIT) training: employees can get the information they need to know, when they need to know it, from the best source, regardless of geography. From an organizational standpoint, technology-based training offers tremendous flexibility and cost savings because employees do not necessarily have to travel to participate in the training medium.

Evaluating Training Programs

Training involves many valuable options and venues, and it's important for an organization to effectively evaluate a training program in advance to ensure that it meets specific criteria. In particular, a training program should be:

▶ **Relevant**

Training programs must be relevant to the needs of employees in the context of improving or advancing their skills and knowledge and achieving organizational objectives. If the training is not relevant, it's a waste of time and resources for both the employee and the organization.

▶ **Ongoing**

Because change is inevitable and constant, employee training must be supported on an ongoing basis and not just at the time of hire. Ongoing training offers many benefits, including an engaged and talented workforce and improved productivity.

▶ **Effective**

Training programs should include a system of checks and balances in order to monitor, measure, and benefit from what is learned. In a traditional classroom environment, test scores might be used. For technology-based training, both the training process and the performance results might be captured and transmitted digitally to validate the organization's *return on investment* (ROI).

▶ **Interesting and enjoyable**

Because people learn differently, it's important to align learning techniques with learning styles to ensure that each employee is engaged and is developing the desired skills and knowledge by participating in the training program. Involving the employee in establishing a plan for meeting ongoing training objectives can be helpful. Also, staying in tune with what employees have found to be valuable in the past can be useful.

While the training must ultimately be applicable to the real work environment, it must also be appealing to learners. It should reflect a diverse set of learning styles and techniques—such as interactive activities, written exercises, discussions, and multiple platforms—that will keep learners interested and engaged.

There are many benefits to supporting and maintaining a well-trained team, including improved motivation and performance and advanced operational efficiencies. To help keep the training process effective, be sure to periodically evaluate your team's training interests and needs. Involve team members as training facilitators when appropriate. Doing so can help build an employee's confidence and presentation skills, as well as mutual respect among team members.

HOW SUPPORTIVE OF TRAINING ARE YOU?

Your attitude, knowledge, and technique will influence how well a training program is implemented and maintained. Review the following recommendations to ensure a healthy return on your training investment.

Place a checkmark (✔) if you already do what is suggested, and an X if you plan to begin this practice.

I normally:

❑ Engage each employee in a periodic performance review, and identify training opportunities.

❑ Discuss with employees their individual growth objectives and organizational objectives to ensure appropriate training strategies.

❑ Before scheduled training, review the training objectives with employees, determining what the outcomes should be and how they will be measured.

❑ Coordinate work flows between team members so that employees away on training can focus on learning, without sacrificing productivity.

❑ Help employees align training objectives with actual job performance.

❑ After they have participated in a training program, ask employees for feedback to determine if other team members could benefit from a presentation or from attending the training program themselves.

❑ Facilitate opportunities for employees to apply what they have learned in their work on a regular basis.

❑ Recognize employees for performance improvements that are the result of new skills and techniques obtained and applied through training.

Promoting Teamwork Through Your Leadership Style

Anyone can manage a group of people, but it takes a leader to facilitate collaboration among team members to bring about innovations and efficiencies for the benefit of both the team and the organization. By fostering mutual trust and respect, a team leader can keep employees motivated and focused. Just as athletes often work hard to perform for a respected coach, employees will value and work hard for a team leader who fosters an environment where everyone adds value and everyone is valued.

Consider the following three approaches to management, and ask yourself which approach best fits your leadership style.

▶ **"I know best."**

This leadership style involves exercising control over others to achieve objectives. Employees are told what to do, how to do it, and when to stop. Employees are also clear on what they did wrong, what they did right, where they are weak, and where they are strong. Based on the self-perception that "I know best," this leadership style reflects someone who views himself or herself as having superior knowledge and ability.

Not surprisingly, this style often limits the exchange of new ideas, suppresses individual development, fosters conflict, hinders collaboration, and encourages inter-group competition. Alternative approaches are limited because communications are one-way.

▶ **"I'll set the goals; you meet them."**

Taking the "I know best" leadership style to another level, this style assumes that because of the leader's superior knowledge, ability, and experience, it's best to set the goals for others to meet. Employees may discuss how they might approach different tasks, but overall performance objectives are non-negotiable.

In this situation, employees tend to lack commitment because there is little to no opportunity for establishing shared outcomes.

▶ **"Let's review the work together, establish realistic goals, and evaluate performance accordingly."**

This leadership style focuses on achieving organizational objectives while engaging employees in determining how the work will be done, what resources will be required, and when success will be rewarded. Leadership is a viewed as a process of facilitation versus authoritative rule. The leader acts as an enabler, rather than as a judge. Communication is open and flows in both directions. Mutual respect and collaboration are valued.

> *Hold yourself responsible for a higher standard than anybody else expects of you. Never excuse yourself."*
>
> **–Henry Ward Beecher**

While it might be obvious that the most effective leadership style involves working together to establish and meet goals, everyone can have bad days. The important focus for a team leader is to know the difference between having a bad day and identifying when it's time to improve one's leadership skills.

"Hal, this team needs a guy with special skills like yours."

CASE STUDY: The Complaining Employees

Danita and John work in data processing under Kim's supervision. They are both unhappy about their current work situations and have been complaining to each other.

Danita is unhappy because Kim never provided her with a job description, and therefore she is unclear about her responsibilities. When she asked Kim about it, she was told, "Don't worry, I'll keep you busy." The reality is that Kim does not like to give Danita new projects until she is finished with her current project. Because Kim is often busy, she does not always assign Danita a new project in good time, often leaving Danita without work for days.

Recently, Danita started helping a co-worker because she had nothing else to do. When Kim noticed this, she took her aside and said, "Don't do that again. Assigning work is my responsibility." Because of complying with Kim's request, Danita has been criticized by her co-workers for not pitching in when they are busy and she is not.

John, on the other hand, is concerned about the backlog building up in his work. The problem is the result of repeated changes in project objectives that were not made clear to him. Kim insists on being the interface for all communications between her department and other departments whenever project objectives are interdependent. Because Kim is so busy, she frequently fails to pass along important information to John, and she is equally slow in passing along John's responses to others.

Are John's and Danita's complaints justified?   ❑ Yes   ❑ No

Why or why not?

_____

_____

_____

_____

Compare your answers to the authors' responses in the Appendix.

Part Summary

Achieving team goals requires qualified, motivated people. As a team leader, you will select team members and guide them in working well with each other. When you're recruiting team members, it helps to understand the personalities involved so that you can build a team that will collaborate effectively to achieve organizational objectives.

While each personality style offers advantages and disadvantages, the objective of the team leader is to leverage the upside of each personality style when managing outcomes. The key is to know what ingredients you have, and how they behave and interact, and then combine them accordingly to achieve the desired results.

Anyone can manage a group of people, but it takes a leader to facilitate collaboration among team members to bring about innovations and efficiencies for the benefit of both the team and the organization. An effective team leader will keep employees motivated and focused by fostering mutual trust and respect.

Building Bridges
to Better
Communication

Individual commitment to a group effort—that is what makes a team work, a company work, a society work, a civilization work."

—Vince Lombardi

In this part:

▶ Facilitating Open Communication

▶ Fostering Teamwork Through Collaboration

▶ Involving the Team in Setting Goals and Standards

▶ Making Problem Solving a Team Effort

▶ Creating a Climate for Team Problem Solving

▶ Examining Conflict

▶ Conflict Resolution Styles

▶ Helping a Team Resolve Conflicts Productively

Facilitating Open Communication

With a solid team framework in place to help you identify, recruit, and assemble a team, you will now focus on building and maintaining open communications. Open communications are vital to collaboration, not only within your team, but also in interactions with other people outside the team and outside the organization. Think of this process as building bridges between two or more people. The strength of the bridge is reflected in the foundation of mutual trust and respect attained through open communications.

For a leader, it's often more important to understand others than it is to be understood. Through developing listening skills, thinking before speaking, and being sensitive to employee behavioral styles, you'll find that your communications are more productive and employees are more productive in their work. Research has shown a positive correlation between effective communication and:

- ▶ Higher levels of productivity
- ▶ Enhanced problem solving
- ▶ Employee satisfaction
- ▶ Process advancements
- ▶ Healthier working relationships
- ▶ Increased collaboration and social capital

Two-Way Communication

Two-way communication involves both listening and speaking. For a team leader, this is critical because you're often the person entrusted with the responsibility of gathering, processing, and transmitting information essential to the well-being of the organization and the team. You need to be able to facilitate two-way communication, both written and oral, between peers, superiors, customers, vendors, investors, and other stakeholders.

In the following table, the left column introduces typical questions from a team member's perspective. In the right column are typical questions from a team leader's perspective. Understanding the subtle differences between the two can help you become a more effective listener, communicator, and leader.

Team Member	Team Leader
▶ What information do I need to provide to my superior(s)?	▶ What information must I have available to support organizational objectives?
▶ Where does my information come from?	▶ How do I best convey information to support objectives?
▶ When do I need to make information available?	▶ How often must I communicate up the ladder to keep everyone informed?
▶ Where can I get specific information about policies and procedures?	▶ Who is depending on me for accurate and timely information?
▶ How do I get this information?	▶ What information do these people need?
▶ What does this information mean to me and my position?	▶ When must I provide them with this information?
▶ Do my colleagues have information that I need?	▶ How might I best provide this information?
▶ How can I facilitate information exchanges among my colleagues?	▶ What information will help my team perform optimally?
▶ How often do information exchanges need to occur?	▶ How might I best share information with my team?
▶ What is the most productive use of this information in my work?	▶ When is it appropriate to delegate information sharing?

Encourage team members to review their own communication skills by using the following exercise. Promote dialogue in ways that promote better communication skills.

REVIEW YOUR COMMUNICATION SKILLS

Complete the following statements by circling the more appropriate choice.

1. Communication is more easily understood by the receiving party when:
   a) You use your full command of the language.
   b) The communication is sent in terms that the receiver will understand.

2. When you're sharing complex information, it is helpful to:
   a) Promote understanding by using specific examples and analogies.
   b) Tell the listener to pay careful attention.

3. You can help people remember key concepts introduced by:
   a) Using repetition to reinforce them.
   b) Expressing yourself clearly.

4. Organizing what you want to say before you say it:
   a) Often takes more time than it is worth.
   b) Promotes better understanding.

5. To ensure that the receiver of the communication understands what the sender is saying:
   a) Ask the receiver if he understands.
   b) Ask the receiver to describe what he thinks was being said.

6. Listening is more effective when you:
   a) Concentrate on the sender and what is being said.
   b) Anticipate what the speaker is going to say.

7. Understanding is easier when you:
   a) Suspend judgment until the sender finishes the message.
   b) Assume that you know the sender's position, and judge accordingly.

8. Understanding can be improved when the receiving party:
   a) Periodically paraphrases what she believes the sender is conveying.
   b) Interrupts the sender to express her viewpoint.

CONTINUED

=== CONTINUED ===

9. Good listeners:
   a) Have their responses ready when the sender stops talking.
   b) Ask questions when they don't understand.

10. Sending and receiving are enhanced when:
    a) Both parties remain attentive and listen.
    b) Both parties enthusiastically talk at the same time.

Compare your answers with the authors' responses in the Appendix.

"Let's go around the room, and talk about the edgy,
creative things we've done so far today."

Fostering Teamwork Through Collaboration

The primary benefit of fostering teamwork through collaboration is that you can get more done with less. As the team leader, you can't be everywhere all of the time to monitor all aspects of progress. Your success often depends on your ability to delegate effectively and to motivate your team in ways that will meet or exceed organizational objectives. By promoting teamwork, you are promoting individual and collective ownership of organizational objectives. When everyone has a personal stake in the outcome, a high level of achievement is possible.

Teamwork cannot be forced. It is self-generating and usually develops through a sense of mutual trust, respect, and collaboration between team members. The more individuals feel that their contributions are respected and valued, the more they are willing to work together productively as a team. By engaging people in setting goals, solving problems, and sharing outcomes, you are conveying that you respect and value your team. In turn, you will find that your team members respect and value you as their leader.

Increased Effectiveness from Collaboration

There are many benefits of collaboration. When people are excited about what they're doing, when they believe that they have something to contribute and that their contributions are valued, there are virtually no limits to shared outcomes. Engaged and motivated team members will typically offer new ideas and be eager to exceed expectations.

Collaboration is about building *social capital*—building connections within and between groups of people. When social capital is productive, there is mutual trust and respect between participants. When social capital is destructive, there is often fear between participants. Research has shown a correlation between high levels of social capital in organizations and communities with high levels of engagement, productivity, and shared prosperity.

When people feel like they belong, they can perform without fear of judgment, criticism, or rejection. By fostering a team environment where team members feel like they belong, you will enjoy profound increased efficiencies in achieving organizational objectives.

Encouraging Collaboration Among Your Team Members

The following guidelines can help you build an environment of collaboration for your team:

▶ Be sensitive to the personality differences between your team members, and look for ways to build upon their strengths as they work with each other.

▶ Develop ways to keep team members engaged in collective planning and problem solving. Facilitate the development of shared solutions, and make it easy for team members to celebrate outcomes.

▶ Promote dialogue in ways that foster open communication without judgment or criticism.

▶ Minimize negative influences that make employees fearful about their work, job, or status on the team. Maximize high levels of social capital by fostering mutual trust and respect.

Involving the Team in Setting Goals and Standards

Setting goals and standards is a process that ultimately determines the basis for your organization's success. The core components of strategic planning are knowing what everyone is working toward, what they need to do to get there, and how they will know when they get there.

Involve the team in setting the strategic goals and standards that they will be held accountable to, and you will significantly increase your chances of success. These are the people whom you recruited, trained, and motivated. They are likely to be qualified to contribute to the strategic planning process, and as a result, to be fully committed to achieving stated outcomes.

Before you begin to engage your team in setting strategic goals and standards, first take a closer look at these two terms:

- ▶ *Goals* are statements that clearly identify, describe, and convey the results to be achieved. They must effectively address:

  - ▷ What it is that the team is working toward; e.g., a new product, the delivery of a service, the development of a new technology, the conclusion to a specific experiment, and so forth

  - ▷ When the task is to be completed

  - ▷ The resources that will be assembled to achieve the desired results

- ▶ *Standards* refer to ongoing performance criteria. These are usually expressed in quantitative terms and may include such things as:

  - ▷ Task specifications

  - ▷ Dates and timelines

  - ▷ Budget parameters

  - ▷ Production rates

  - ▷ Design tolerances

  - ▷ Portfolio performance

  - ▷ Sales goals

  - ▷ Burn rates

  - ▷ Consulting hours

  - ▷ Marketing objectives

  - ▷ Safety standards

Goal-Setting Roles for Team Members and Leaders

As with most aspects of a well-functioning team, it takes time and practice to develop a productive approach to setting goals and standards collaboratively. The following table offers examples of various roles that team members and team leaders might play in support of this process.

Team Member	Team Leader
Contributes to establishing strategic goals and standards; understands and accepts responsibility and accountability for outcomes.	Ensures that strategic goals and standards are in line with organizational objectives.
Participates in the development of measurement criteria for monitoring and ensuring progress.	Maintains a balance between individual progress and collective team progress to ensure desired outcomes.
Documents the action items to be performed to attain goals and meet standards.	Facilitates team communications to promote new ideas, innovations, and efficiencies in how the work is performed.
Identifies interdependencies where the performance goals and standards of others affect individual and collective outcomes.	Promotes open communication to maintain motivation, mutual trust, and respect among team members in the process of meeting objectives.
Tracks and reports progress over time, engaging others in collaborative venues to identify and overcome obstacles to ensure results.	Ensures that all team members have the resources they need to achieve individual and collective success in meeting shared objectives.

Team-Building Tip: *A productive team leader is a coach, champion, and facilitator of collaboration, rather than a boss, judge, or authoritative ruler.*

Making Problem Solving a Team Effort

Because change is inevitable and constant, problems will arise that need to be solved. More often than not, problems are the result of a combination of factors rather than a singular event or person. It's virtually impossible for team leaders to take into account all of the factors that contribute to why a problem arises, or all of the paths that might be taken to overcome it.

As a result, problems may become opportunities for a team leader to foster further collaboration among team members. By engaging the team in an ongoing process of identifying problems and solutions, you are conveying your confidence and trust in their ability to overcome obstacles.

You are also not contributing to the problem by micro-managing outcomes. By making problem solving a team effort, you are leveraging the talents of your team in achieving outcomes. If you try to dominate the problem-solving process, you may compromise the team's effectiveness, as well as your own.

The following case study provides an example of engaging a team in solving a problem.

CASE STUDY: The Missing Keys

Renee, a nursing supervisor, was frustrated because the nurses who report to her were constantly losing or misplacing the keys to the medicine cart. Each shift was responsible for a set of keys, which was to be passed on to the next shift. Instead, the keys were too often left in uniform pockets and taken home, or they were simply lost.

Having nurses search for keys was a waste of time. If the keys got into the wrong hands, there were serious ramifications to consider. Whenever the keys were lost, the medicine cart had to have a whole new locking system installed and more keys made; this was expensive and time consuming.

Renee decided to write a memo and distribute it to the nurses on all three shifts. In it, she explained the problem and associated risks and costs, and she invited the nurses to discuss possible solutions and share their ideas during shift meetings.

This approach resulted in the exchange of a variety of ideas, including having the nursing supervisor be responsible for the keys, and making the keys always visible on a nurse's uniform.

After everyone had an opportunity to share their thoughts, a twofold system was implemented. Brightly colored spiral wristbands were purchased and given to each nurse to hold the keys, and a system for signing the keys in and out was implemented.

Although most nurses liked the brightly colored wristbands, some nurses found them to be cumbersome, so they pinned the bands to their uniforms instead. The sign-in system made it much easier to track down missing keys.

Thanks to Renee's approach to problem solving, incidences of missing and lost keys decreased dramatically. Instead of sharing her frustration with her team, she productively engaged her team to develop an effective solution that worked for everyone.

Team-Building Tip: *Never underestimate the willingness and ability of your team to solve problems. Problems can be great opportunities for fostering collaboration and improving efficiency.*

SEVEN STEPS TO SOLVING PROBLEMS

Because problems are inevitable and affect everyone, problem-solving techniques are important skills to develop for all employees. Of the following seven steps to problem-solving, check (✔) those steps that you view as useful in your operation.

_____ 1. **State in general terms what the problem is.** Begin with a general idea of what you consider to be the problem. Avoid being judgmental or too quick to draw conclusions—facts may be revealed that further define the problem.

_____ 2. **Gather the facts.** Engage others in determining what elements are involved in terms of people, processes, and/or technology. Determine where, when, and how the problem occurred. Also determine what is at stake and whether the problem can happen again.

_____ 3. **Restate the problem.** Based on the contributions of others, restate the problem thoroughly and in a context that fosters further collaboration in solving the problem.

_____ 4. **Identify alternative solutions.** Engage others in introducing and discussing ideas. Resist judging any one option until everyone has had an opportunity to contribute.

_____ 5. **Evaluate alternatives.** Engage others in assessing each option's strengths, weaknesses, opportunities, and threats. Determine which option provides the optimum solution, and what is involved in implementation.

_____ 6. **Implement the decision.** Coordinate resources and facilitate the implementation of the agreed-upon solution.

_____ 7. **Monitor and verify the results.** Was the problem solved? To what degree? If not, repeat steps 4–7.

Creating a Climate for Team Problem Solving

A team involved in problem solving can get better results by using sound group processes. This means that team members commit to finding the best possible solution to a problem, rather than imposing their exclusive viewpoint. The leader participates as a team member and is subject to the same rules. Open communication is expected, and team members are encouraged to challenge ideas to test their usefulness in solving the problem. A solution designed by a group is often more successful than a solution offered by an individual.

> *Nature has given us two ears, two eyes, and but one tongue—to the end that we should hear and see more than we speak.*"
>
> –**Socrates**

DOES THE CLIMATE FOSTER PROBLEM SOLVING?

The following conditions support good team problem solving. Check (✔) those that exist now in your team, and write an X next to those you want to add.

_____ 1. Team members readily contribute from their experience and listen to the contributions of others.

_____ 2. Conflicts arising from different points of view are considered helpful and are resolved constructively by the team.

_____ 3. Team members challenge suggestions they believe are unsupported by facts or logic, but avoid arguing just to have it their way.

_____ 4. Inadequate solutions are not supported just for the sake of harmony or agreement.

_____ 5. Differences of opinion are discussed and resolved. Coin tossing, averaging, majority votes, and similar copouts are avoided when making a decision.

_____ 6. Every team member strives to make the problem-solving process efficient and is careful to facilitate rather than hinder discussion.

_____ 7. Team members encourage and support co-workers who might be reluctant to offer ideas.

_____ 8. Team members understand the value of time and work to eliminate extraneous or repetitious discussion.

_____ 9. Team decisions are not arbitrarily overruled by the leader simply because he does not agree with them.

_____ 10. The team understands that the leader will make the best decision she can, if a satisfactory team solution is not forthcoming.

Examining Conflict

Conflicts can arise at any time and under any circumstances whenever two or more people interact. However, conflict is not always a bad thing, as the following example suggests:

▶ To get a head start in the market, a sales manager wants the research and development staff to complete a new design earlier than was originally planned. The CFO wants to stick to the current schedule because it supports cash flow, which is funding R&D. The marketing department needs to know when to begin designing new collaterals to support sales efforts.

In this situation, the participants mean well, and if asked, will maintain that they are trying to accomplish what they perceive to be in the best interests of the organization. Nevertheless, the opportunity for conflict is present because of:

▶ Different perspectives regarding needs, objectives, and values

▶ Different perspectives regarding behavior and communication styles

▶ Different assumptions about priorities and resource allocation

66 *There is no such thing as a problem without a gift for you in its hands. You seek problems because you need their gifts."*

–Richard Bach

Conflict Resolution Styles

When conflict does occur in an organization, the results will be positive or negative, depending on how the conflict is dealt with. From this perspective, a team leader can have a profound effect on managing outcomes based on how well she or he responds. The following table describes five basic approaches to conflict resolution.

Behavior Style	Characteristics	Justification
Avoidance	Non-confrontational. Ignores conflicts, or denies that a conflict exists.	If I get involved, I might add to the conflict. If I pretend it's not there, it might go away.
Accommodating	Agreeable, nonassertive. Cooperative at the expense of outcomes.	I don't want to risk not being liked or adding to the conflict.
Win/lose	Confrontational and aggressive.	It's about moving on. If they are going to behave like children, I'm going to have to treat them like children.
Compromising	Somewhere amidst the conflict is the right answer. Assess, judge, divide and conquer to move on.	I believe that everyone's viewpoint has something to offer. I'll decide what needs to be given up in order to get on with progress.
Problem solving	Facilitate productive debate in which individual interests are voiced. Collaboration reinforces relationship integrity, and cooperation supports shared outcomes.	I believe everyone cares about the outcome. With the right approach, I can facilitate collaboration so that everyone benefits.

As you can see from the above options, conflict can become unhealthy when a solution is either forced or not addressed at all. However, with a little investment of time and an ability to listen, a team leader can bring about positive change in ways that respect people's differences and actually leverage these differences in bringing about transformative and productive change.

Helping a Team Resolve Conflicts Productively

Helping members of your team to understand that not all conflict is bad will help them to view and embrace differences in ways that can lead to innovations and operational breakthroughs. Use the following diagram to discuss ways in which conflicts can be resolved productively for all parties involved.

Think about what style you use when faced with conflict. Place the letter "M" in the area of the diagram that best describes your style when you're dealing with conflicts among members of your team. Place a "P" near the style you use when dealing with conflicts among your peers, and place an "S" near the style you use when dealing with your superiors. Correlate the preceding table with this diagram, and look for ways you might improve your conflict resolution skills. Use a similar approach with your team members to assist them with improving their skills.

REVIEWING BEHAVIOR STYLES

Using what you've learned about the five basic behavior styles for approaching conflict (Avoidance, Accommodating, Win/Lose, Compromising, and Problem Solving), review and respond to the following questions.

1. Which style pretends that there is no conflict?

   _____

2. Which style leverages everyone's interests and works to facilitate shared outcomes?

   _____

3. Which style is agreeable, nonassertive, and cooperative at the expense of outcomes?

   _____

4. Which behavior style is the most confrontational and aggressive?

   _____

5. Which style takes into account everyone's viewpoint to form an independent decision?

   _____

Compare your answers with the authors' responses in the Appendix.

Team-Building Tip: *Conflict is necessary and healthy when it causes the parties to explore new ideas, test their positions and beliefs, and stretch their imaginations. When conflict is dealt with constructively, people can be stimulated to greater creativity, which leads to a wider variety of alternatives and better results.*

When team members understand the nature of conflict and use constructive methods for resolving conflict, they can usually work out disagreements themselves. In situations where they need help, or when a situation calls for intervention by the team leader, you should proactively facilitate collaboration to bring about a solution. For example, consider how you might you solve the following conflict.

CASE STUDY: Conflicting Team Members

Rakesha is the supervisor of a quality-control team in a chemical production facility. Current practice requires that all testing results be reported to the administrative office. The problem with this rule is that it does not always allow for timely and necessary adjustments in quality control for problems that have been reported.

Two members of her quality-control team have approached her separately with different ideas. Joe wants to send the results to the foreman in charge of the unit that produced the samples that are being tested. Angela wants to send the reports directly to the lead operator of the unit, with the idea that he would have the authority to implement corrective action immediately.

Both Joe and Angela are responsible and productive employees, but they are also highly competitive. Rakesha is aware that they have exchanged a few pointed remarks on this issue. Both ideas are reasonable, and either approach will be an improvement over the current practice.

Review each scenario below and choose which of the five behavioral styles best matches the approach used. Write your choice on the line provided to the left of the scenario. Then check (✓) which of the five scenarios you would use if you were Rakesha.

WL = Win/Lose   AV = Avoidance   AC = Accommodation
CO = Compromising   PS = Problem Solving

❑ 1. _____ Study the situation independently and decide who is right and who is wrong. Then tell Joe and Angela to implement your decision.

❑ 2. _____ Wait to see what happens.

❑ 3. _____ Cooperate with whatever Angela or Joe end up doing so as not to add to the conflict.

❑ 4. _____ Get Joe and Angela together so that they can each explain to you why their idea is better. Based on what you learn, choose the best approach.

❑ 5. _____ Sit down with Joe and Angela. Facilitate a brainstorming session in which ideas are written down, reviewed, and selected together based on the best interests of the organization.

Compare your answers with the authors' responses in the Appendix.

Part Summary

By listening, thinking before speaking, and being sensitive to employee behavioral styles, you'll find that your communications are more productive, and employees are more productive in their work. For a team leader, this is critical because you're often the person entrusted with the responsibility for gathering, processing, and transmitting information essential to the well-being of the organization and the team.

Collaboration is also critical. Your success often depends on your ability to delegate effectively and to motivate your team in ways that will meet or exceed organizational objectives. By promoting teamwork, you are promoting individual and collective ownership of organizational objectives. When everyone has a personal stake in the outcome, a high level of achievement is possible.

Involve the team in setting the strategic goals and standards that they will be held accountable for, and you will significantly increase your chances of success. Also, engage the team in an ongoing process of identifying problems and solutions. Doing so will convey your confidence and trust in the team's ability to overcome obstacles. A solution designed by a group is often more successful than a solution offered by an individual.

If members of your team understand that conflict is often an opportunity, they can view and embrace differences in ways that can lead to innovations and operational breakthroughs. When team members understand the nature of conflict and use constructive methods for resolving conflicts, they can usually work out disagreements themselves. When they need help, or when a situation calls for intervention by the team leader, you should proactively facilitate collaboration to bring about a solution.

Ensuring Mutual

Trust and Respect

We make a living by what we get. We make a life by what we give."

–Winston Churchill

In this part:

- ▶ Fostering an Environment of Trust
- ▶ Recognizing Employee Performance
- ▶ Implementing Positive Discipline
- ▶ Coaching: Essential in Team Building
- ▶ Six Tools for Effective Coaching

Fostering an Environment of Trust

Trust is a key ingredient of a healthy relationship. When people feel safe in each other's company, they can focus their energy on being creative, productive, and collaborative. When people feel threatened, they tend to keep to themselves and do the minimum work required. Which type of employee would you like to have working on your team?

Trust must be earned—it is the result of patterns of behavior between two or more people over time. The more each person believes that his views are valued, the more comfortable he will feel expressing them. If he fears being derided or ignored, his contributions will be limited. Trust does not mean that everyone must always agree, of course.

Each individual brings something unique and special to the team as a result of her experiences, skill sets, knowledge, and personality. By fostering trust within the team, a team leader builds an environment where differences between team members can be valued and respected for what they offer the team.

Trust affects virtually every aspect of team performance. Without it, employee behavior tends to focus on self-interest. In an environment of trust, employees will willingly and proactively interact, seeking ways to learn from each other, develop new ideas, contribute to mutually productive outcomes, and share success.

Elements of Trust

In the following table are comments from workshop participants who were asked to describe their views on trust in the context of workplace team-building.

Individual	Elements of Trust
A	"To build trust, it's essential to have clearly and consistently administered goals that involve employee input. Employees must perceive their managers as open, fair, honest, and willing to listen. Managers must be decisive and stand by their decisions in difficult situations." "Employees must have the confidence that their manager will support them, even in delicate matters, and take responsibility for group actions. A manager must also readily give credit to employees when credit is due."
B	"I define trust as an assured reliance on the character, ability, and strength or truth of someone or something. Trust is built in a work group by promoting open communications, providing fair leadership, and supervising with sensitivity."
C	"Establishing trust in a work group requires open and honest communication, accepting others, sharing a common goal, and respecting the opinions of others on how to achieve that goal."
D	"Trust is necessary to having a productive working environment. It is essential for all personnel to practice open, honest communication to increase awareness and build cooperation. Trust promotes loyalty and commitment to achieving the organization's goals and objectives."

Recognizing Employee Performance

The desire to belong to something is part of human nature. People want to feel welcome and accepted as a part of a team—they want a sense of belonging to something important. Recognizing employees for a job well done reinforces their sense of belonging and encourages continued high performance in the future.

Objective employee-recognition practices are often the most effective. These practices include using standard systems, forms, and policies to assess project performance periodically and to assess overall performance at different times throughout the year. Recognition that is not objective, such as praise, can be less effective because it exists outside of any formal framework and therefore can be taken away just as casually.

"Hey, by the way, good team play on the dinosaur hunt today."

In addition to having formal recognition policies and procedures, it's important to encourage and practice good manners among team members. Manners include common courtesies, such as saying "please" and "thank you" in communication exchanges. Comments such as "good job" or "nice work" are also valuable forms of recognition that reflect team members' appreciation for each other's contributions.

Periodically using objective forms of recognition and routinely practicing good manners are reliable ways to recognize employees for positive work performance. The following table introduces forms of recognition behavior and leadership styles. Think about your own style, as well as the styles of your team members, as you review this information, and identify any areas that may require improvement.

Which Team Leader Will You Be?

Constructive	Destructive
Helping people feel like they belong.	Being insensitive to the needs and interests of others.
Using objective forms of employee recognition periodically and consistently.	Casually practicing subjective forms of employee recognition only to get something in return.
Practicing good manners and expressing friendly greetings on a routine basis.	Failing to practice good manners, or failing to express casual greetings on a routine basis.
Proactively reinforcing positive performance.	Embarrassing employees by publically judging and criticizing their work, and using body language to show disapproval or disgust.
Facilitating recognition among team members in the form of good manners.	Being divisive by choosing favorites among the team and giving preferential treatment.
Add from your own experience: _____ _____ _____ _____	Add from your own experience: _____ _____ _____ _____

Team-Building Tip: *Objective forms of recognition and good manners go a long way in reinforcing positive employee performance.*

For more information on providing recognition, read the Crisp Series book *Retaining Your Employees,* by Barb Wingfield and Janice Berry.

Implementing Positive Discipline

Discipline is a necessity in virtually all aspects of life. Although diversity can be a productive element of team productivity, diversity of performance is not productive if people are failing to contribute their share or are behaving disruptively. When this occurs, it's important for a team leader to implement positive forms of discipline. Failure to take productive action condones such behavior.

Effective discipline requires an effective approach from the team leader and a receptive attitude from the team member. In this context, attitude equates to maturity level. Team members with low maturity levels will require a team leader who can provide a high level of structure, while team members with a high maturity level will require less structure.

ASSESS YOUR PROFICIENCY

Below are specific disciplinary techniques that team leaders can apply with team members as necessary. As maturity levels vary, the degree to which the technique is implemented may vary. Indicate your proficiency with each technique by checking (✔) the appropriate box.

Do Well	Should Improve	
❑	❑	1. Consistently engaging team members in setting goals and standards to ensure mutual understanding and to support performance.
❑	❑	2. Monitoring performance and collaborating with team members to ensure high levels of performance.
❑	❑	3. Providing encouragement to support the attainment of mutual goals and objectives.
❑	❑	4. Employing formal performance assessment procedures to recognize and document the achievement of goals and standards, or to address problem areas.
❑	❑	5. Proactively and routinely practicing and encouraging good manners among all team members.
❑	❑	6. When documented problems have not been corrected, jointly defining in writing the consequences that will result if corrective action is not taken.

Coaching: Essential in Team Building

Coaching a team in an organizational setting is similar to coaching a sports team. Each member of the sports team offers different skills and performs different functions in order to win the game. In the workplace, each employee offers different skills and performs different functions to support the sustainability of the organization. Good coaching skills are what make all of this work.

Coaching is about crafting and fully understanding a game plan, or plan of action, understanding each position on the team, pulling together the right skills and talent to fill those positions, and implementing a strategy that leads to results. As the team meets its rivals, the coach must adapt strategies and tactics, refining and maintaining performance accordingly.

Coaching and Organizational Leadership

Coaching is a primary component of organizational leadership. Historical approaches to management in industrial settings often required authoritative, highly structured forms of leadership because the work was task oriented and risks were high whenever dangerous machinery was involved.

Today's work is more knowledge based and service oriented, and therefore requires a different style of leadership. It's not so much about managing the process of productivity as it is about facilitating employee skill development, motivation, and collaboration so that employees drive results.

With effective coaching, a team leader challenges employees to do their best. By effectively delegating, a team leader fosters skills development and the assuming of responsibility for performance outcomes. By providing employees with opportunities to grow and learn, a team leader facilitates innovation and productivity, thereby increasing the chances of success for the individual, the team, and the organization.

Mentoring: A Strategy for Growth

Many people remember someone who had a profound effect in their lives. Mentors are people who, consciously or not, take an interest in the development of another person in a way that has a lasting and positive effect. In a Crisp book titled *Making the Most of Being Mentored*, Stephen Gianotti introduces the many ways that people can serve as mentors to help employe CONTINUED higher levels of productivity in the workplace.

Every team leader has an opportunity to function as a mentor. The most direct form of mentoring is leading by example. Demonstrating integrity, setting high standards of performance, and consistently achieving stated outcomes are characteristics you can encourage in others through your own behavior.

A mentor takes the time to focus on a person's interests and needs, providing support and encouragement to help the person develop skills and advance in his or her career. Assisting team members in this way is fundamental to individual growth and to organizational success.

IDENTIFYING SPHERES OF INFLUENCE

Most managers can identify people who have influenced their lives in a positive way—parents, friends, teachers, associates, or colleagues. Sometimes this influence has been profound, perhaps even changing the course of their lives.

Think about the influences in your life and answer the questions in the spaces provided.

Who has had a powerful influence on you?

_____   _____

_____   _____

_____   _____

_____   _____

In what ways were you influenced?

_____

_____

_____

CONTINUED

Who influences you now?

_____ _____

_____ _____

_____ _____

_____ _____

In what ways do these people influence you?

_____

_____

_____

Whom do you influence?

_____ _____

_____ _____

_____ _____

_____ _____

What outcomes do you have the power to influence?

_____

_____

Applying coaching techniques to improve the performance of individual team members, the team, and the organization as a whole can bring about transformative organizational change and lasting positive results.

Team-Building Tip: *When two or more people come together routinely to interact, there will be a need for mutually defined and honored rules of engagement.*

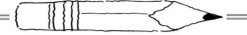

WHAT'S YOUR ATTITUDE TOWARD COACHING?

Review the following coaching applications and for each one, indicate your former attitude and current perspective toward coaching, using the scale below.

E = Essential   U = Useful   W = Waste of Time

Coaching Applications	Former Attitude	Current Perspective
Coaching encourages employees to perform their very best.		
Coaching involves developing employee skills to improve individual and collective team performance.		
Coaching builds teamwork; employees understand that they are part of a bigger objective and that collaboration is important to shared success.		
Employees respond well to being part of a team when a coach keeps them engaged in the planning process and helps them develop the skills required to succeed.		
Coaching includes motivating, mentoring, and celebrating shared success to drive future outcomes.		

Six Tools for Effective Coaching

Effective coaching offers many benefits to the team leader, team members, and the organization. When a team is working seamlessly to overcome obstacles, meet deadlines, and manage change, the organization thrives. In a thriving organization, job security, career advancement, and employee recognition expand.

In the Crisp book *Coaching for Development,* Marianne Minor presents the following tips to help team leaders develop effective coaching techniques. Review these tips to assess your own coaching skills:

► **Listen**

▷ Pay attention to employees when they are speaking.

▷ Be attentive, minimize distractions, and be conscious of your body language.

▷ Repeat what you understand the employee to be conveying. Use examples and analogies, and ask open-ended questions.

▷ Pay attention to the person's body language and other communication signals.

▷ Summarize your understanding and ask for confirmation at the end of the exchange.

► **Observe**

▷ Look for indications that the employee needs help or is ready to assume more responsibility.

▷ Watch for any changes in performance, and be prepared to respond.

▷ Take note of employee behavioral styles with others.

▷ Provide opportunities for employees to develop skills, expand performance capacities, and overcome obstacles.

► **Analyze**

▷ Collaborate in assessing problems and implementing solutions.

▷ Mutually define improvement areas, such as technical skill sets, motivation, or interpersonal skills.

▷ Be sensitive to employee behaviors, motivators, and learning styles.

▶ **Interview**

▷ Routinely engage employees in assessing skill sets, performance standards, and accomplishments.

▷ Use a collaborative and open communication style that fosters cooperation and honesty.

▷ Leverage established organizational policies and practices to capture employee perspectives on strategic goals, standards, and performance.

▶ **Contract**

▷ Create and leverage organizational systems to document and agree on the nature of the employee-employer relationship.

▷ Encourage and empower employees to take a proactive role in their career development.

▷ Be clear about expectations regarding employee accountability, and put in writing the details (who, what, when, how) to ensure employee ownership and responsibility for outcomes.

▶ **Provide feedback**

▷ Practice good manners and use objective forms of recognition to provide feedback about employee performance.

▷ Tailor the message to the audience to avoid overwhelming or confusing employees.

▷ Incorporate the following nine tips for providing effective feedback:

1. Avoid personal opinions and drama.

2. Prepare the employee ahead of time by sharing the framework for the feedback process.

3. Ensure that feedback content is in context by aligning comments with specific, agreed-upon performance objectives.

4. Remain focused on organizational objectives.

5. Avoid using labels, stereotyping, criticism, and judgment.

6. Convey how performance relates to outcomes that affect the individual, the team, and the organization.

7. Introduce feedback in the form of a question to avoid putting the employee on the defensive.

8. Ask the employee to summarize his understanding of the exchange.

9. Provide an opportunity to ask questions during and following the exchange.

CASE STUDY: Putting Coaches to Work

Darryl was a new employee with great potential. Lucinda, his manager, was thrilled to have someone new in her department with so much experience in the industry. Lucinda was excited about what this experience represented to the overall performance of her team, and she wanted to put Darryl's expertise to use as quickly as possible.

To ensure that Darryl and the organization were on the same page, Lucinda called a meeting with him to discuss and establish strategic goals and performance standards. During the meeting, Lucinda invited Darryl to share with her some of his experiences in his prior position, including what he liked and what he didn't like about his former work environment. She listened intently as he explained.

As Lucinda continued to observe and to listen carefully to Darryl's comments, she perceived that he was a strong team player who valued collaboration.

However, shortly after this meeting, Lucinda noticed that Darryl was not performing up to the standards that they had agreed on. She discussed this with him by using open-ended questions, and she discovered that Darryl was holding back—he often felt reluctant to contribute his expertise and knowledge because he did not want to alienate his new co-workers.

With this new level of understanding, Lucinda explained to Darryl why his expertise was vital to the team's performance and effectiveness. She also described how organizational policies and practices were used to recognize individual and collective team performance. As the weeks progressed, Darryl learned firsthand not only that his skills were useful to the team, but also that other team members offered skills that helped him to improve as well.

By taking into account Darryl's needs and the needs of the team, and by employing sound communication skills, Lucinda was able to advance mutual trust and respect among her team members while bringing about the performance advancements she had hoped for when hiring Darryl.

For more information on coaching, read the Crisp Series book *Coaching for Development* by Marianne Minor.

RATE YOUR SKILLS AS A COACH

Use the following scale to assess your own coaching skills. Ask your team members to rate you as well, and compare the results.

> 5 = Outstanding   4 = Very Good   3 = Satisfactory
> 2 = Needs Improvement   1 = Poor

1. I am sensitive to differences in employee behaviors and coach each person accordingly.   5 4 3 2 1

2. I encourage employee input regarding ways to improve team performance.   5 4 3 2 1

3. I empower employees to solve their own problems.   5 4 3 2 1

4. I collaborate with employees to ensure mutual understanding of goals and performance standards.   5 4 3 2 1

5. I provide constructive feedback about employee performance.   5 4 3 2 1

6. I help employees plan their career objectives.   5 4 3 2 1

7. I understand what motivates each of my employees.   5 4 3 2 1

8. I provide opportunities for employee growth.   5 4 3 2 1

9. I facilitate collaboration among team members.   5 4 3 2 1

10. I encourage employees to resolve conflicts, and I facilitate problem solving when necessary.   5 4 3 2 1

11. I foster a team environment of mutual respect and trust.   5 4 3 2 1

A score below 4 in any of these areas suggests room for improvement.

Part Summary

In an environment of trust, employees interact more willingly and proactively, seeking ways to learn from each other, develop new ideas, contribute to mutually productive outcomes, and share success.

In addition to fostering a sense of trust in your team, it's important to establish a recognition policy. Recognizing employees for a job well done reinforces their sense of belonging and encourages continued high performance.

Also important is a sense of discipline. Effective discipline requires an effective team leadership approach and receptive attitudes among team members.

Coaching is about crafting and fully understanding a game plan, understanding each position on the team, pulling together the right skills and talent to fill those positions, and implementing a strategy that leads to results.

Every team leader has an opportunity to act as a mentor. The most direct form of mentoring is leading by example. Demonstrating integrity, setting high standards of performance, and consistently achieving agreed-upon outcomes are characteristics you can encourage in others through your own behavior.

A P P E N D I X

Assessing Your Progress

Answer the following true/false questions to review what you have learned.

True   False

❏   ❏   1. Team leaders engage team members in establishing goals and standards, and then collaborate to monitor progress and performance outcomes.

❏   ❏   2. When you assemble a strong team that works well together, there is little need to improve your own skills.

❏   ❏   3. People are more productive when they feel a sense of belonging and are valued for their ideas and contributions.

❏   ❏   4. Individual success and team success are interrelated.

❏   ❏   5. Recruiting qualified people who work well with others will support team building.

❏   ❏   6. It is not important to involve employees in planning or in setting goals or performance standards related to their work.

❏   ❏   7. Team leaders facilitate the training of team members and practice coaching techniques to help them apply what has been learned in the work environment.

❏   ❏   8. Teams work more effectively when communications are open, feedback is objective, and there is a high level of fear.

❏   ❏   9. Trust is a minor factor in most team situations.

❏   ❏   10. Team members need to know everything that affects the work they are doing.

❏   ❏   11. Competition and conflict in a team are often healthy.

❏   ❏   12. Mentoring employees supports organizational growth.

❏   ❏   13. The objectives of the organization take precedence over the objectives of the individual.

❏   ❏   14. Successful teams have little need for recognition or rewards.

❏   ❏   15. Discipline is a necessity in virtually all aspects of teamwork.

Check your answers against the authors' responses on the next page.

Assessing Your Progress

1. True. Establishing objectives and monitoring performance together are critical to ensuring outcomes.

2. False. Teams are dynamic. As environmental factors change, a team leader must respond to ensure that the team stays motivated and productive.

3. True. When people feel that they belong and are valued, they are likely to perform better.

4. True. In a true team environment, success is about both individual and collective outcomes.

5. True. Good people are the foundation of organizational success.

6. False. Failing to engage employees in the nature of their work and how it will be measured hinders them in taking responsibility for outcomes.

7. True. A team leader is responsible for ensuring that an employee is trained and that what is learned ultimately benefits the organization.

8. False. While open communications and objective feedback are important components of team performance, fear is a more powerful and destructive force.

9. False. Trust is one of the most vital ingredients in team effectiveness.

10. True. The more forthright, comprehensive, and accurate a team leader can be in providing team members with information about their work, the easier it will be to get the work done.

11. False. Competition and conflict are usually destructive in a team environment.

12. True. Mentoring can be an effective and powerful tool to help employees grow and thereby contribute to the vitality of the organization.

13. True. By ensuring its own success, the organization will be able to provide jobs, training, and individual and collective forms of reward and recognition.

14. False. Recognition and rewards promote a sense of mutual respect and value, and serve as strong motivators.

15. True. When two or more people come together on a routine basis to interact, there will be a need for mutually defined and honored rules of engagement.

Ten Ways to Construct a Strong Team

This book on team building has addressed many of the components needed to build a successful team, including planning, organization, goal setting, motivation, conflict resolution, problem solving, and coaching. Place a check (✔) next to the items that you intend to employ or that you have already employed successfully.

❑   1. Using planning techniques to help build a team.

❑   2. Aligning organizational needs with recruiting practices.

❑   3. Mutually establishing strategic goals and performance standards.

❑   4. Empowering employees to take responsibility for their career growth.

❑   5. Ensuring adequate resources to foster individual and collective performance improvements.

❑   6. Practicing and encouraging the use of good manners.

❑   7. Providing routine and objective feedback.

❑   8. Fostering a team environment of mutual trust and respect.

❑   9. Leveraging established formal policies and practices to recognize and reward performance.

❑   10. Documenting disciplinary practices and mutually defining corrective action in writing to promote improvement and minimize turnover.

Reflect on what you have learned, and then develop a personal action plan, using the guide on the next page.

Developing a Personal Action Plan

Use the following statements to develop a personal action plan that demonstrates your commitment to improving your leadership skills.

1. My current team-building skills are effective in the following areas:

   _____

   _____

2. I want to improve my team-building skills in the following areas:

   _____

   _____

3. My goals for improving my team-building skills are as follows (be sure they are specific, attainable, and measurable):

   _____

   _____

4. The following people and resources can help me achieve my goals:

   _____

   _____

5. The following action items and timelines will help me track and monitor my progress as I work toward these objectives:

   _____

   _____

Appendix to Part 1

Comments & Suggested Responses

Case Study: Can This Manager Be Saved?

Chris is in trouble. The good news is that she recognizes it. While it appears that she has her own work requirements to fill, she recognizes that overall productivity relies on the collective performance of the group. Instead of viewing staff members according to their individual job descriptions and distinct functions, she has an opportunity to build a team.

Currently, her staff members seem to view themselves as individuals within a group that was assembled for organizational reasons, rather than as members of a team. Poor performance and infighting may be the result of their not understanding their individual and collective roles within the bigger picture of organizational objectives.

By being proactive instead of reactive, Chris has an opportunity to significantly improve performance. She can pull her group together to facilitate dialogue about current perceptions of work and how each position relates to the others. By engaging individuals in the process of productive change, she can build mutual trust and respect for new ideas and the unique talents that each person has to offer toward achieving shared goals.

How can Chris achieve all this and more? That is the purpose of this book.

Appendix to Part 2

Comments & Suggested Responses

Case Study: Which Leadership Style Would You Prefer?

It's useful that both Morgan and Aiden recognize the importance and value of planning and establishing clear goals.

Team members who have limited knowledge or experience might appreciate Morgan's approach because she offers a lot of structure, and they can benefit from that. As they develop their own knowledge and skills over time, however, they might begin to feel restricted and afraid to share new ideas. Morgan's style of control might also hinder open communications, as well as the development of new efficiencies and other operational innovations, because there is little room for creativity.

Experienced members of the team will appreciate Aiden's approach because it provides opportunities for introducing new ideas. His leadership style offers a climate in which individuals are encouraged to develop personally and collectively as a team. Open communications are facilitated because all team members are required to participate in day-to-day planning, organizing, and problem solving. Aiden's employees will further benefit from his decision to participate in a management training program because he will be building upon his natural talent for facilitating mutual respect and collaboration in bringing about shared outcomes.

Appendix to Part 3

Comments & Suggested Responses

Case Study: The Complaining Employees

Danita and John have good reasons to be unhappy. Danita wants to understand what her job expectations are and what might be involved in advancing. She has made an effort to obtain a copy of her job description, but Kim has not responded and has not fulfilled her promise to keep Danita busy. It is natural to become frustrated when those in a position of influence undermine your efforts to succeed in your work or advance your career.

Kim is also undermining John's success by failing to foster open and productive communication between departments. If John cannot develop and maintain a clear understanding of work objectives, he cannot perform effectively. It's natural for John to become frustrated in this situation.

Kim's tendency to micro-manage all aspects of the work in her department is destructive. Her leadership style conveys that she does not believe that Danita and John are capable of managing their own productivity. As a result, the performance of the overall department is suffering. Team members are discouraged from helping each other, and deadlines are not met because critical instructions are not being communicated effectively.

If Kim is to turn the situation around, she will need reevaluate her leadership style and engage her team more proactively.

Appendix to Part 4

Comments & Suggested Responses

Review Your Communication Skills

1. b
2. a
3. a
4. b
5. b
6. a
7. a
8. a
9. b
10. a

Reviewing Behavior Styles

1. Avoidance
2. Problem Solving
3. Accommodating
4. Win/Lose
5. Compromising

Case Study: Conflicting Team Members

1. **WL.** This scenario uses the Win/Lose approach because it takes the conflict-resolution opportunity away from Angela and Joe and makes one of them a loser.

2. **AV.** This scenario uses Avoidance behavior because it is suggesting that you do nothing. Angela and Joe will be left to continue their conflict, while quality-control results will continue to be compromised.

3. **AC.** This scenario demonstrates being an Accommodator at the expense of outcomes. You think this approach will ensure that both Joe and Angela will like you, but it does nothing to resolve the conflict or the problem.

4. **CO.** This scenario uses the Compromise approach. It allows both Angela and Joe to present and defend their ideas, but it also reinforces the idea that the process is competitive instead of collaborative, because something must be given up in order to move forward.

5. **PS.** This scenario uses the Problem-Solving approach. It is the most productive because it facilitates collaboration between Rakesha, Angela, and Joe so that all ideas can be introduced, assessed, and weighed against the interests of the organization, which is the main objective. This approach also helps to shift the focus away from a contest between Angela and Joe, and toward an organizational challenge that, when overcome, offers benefits for everyone involved.

   This approach also results in the best outcome: a new process of sending the quality-control report to the foreman, with a copy also being sent to the lead operator and administrator.

Additional Reading

Crisp Series books:

Van Daele, Carrie. *50 One-Minute Tips for Trainers*.

Bonet, Diana. *The Business of Listening*.

Hackett, Donald, Ph.D. and Charles Martin, Ph.D. *Facilitation Skills for Team Leaders*.

Hayes, David K. and Brother Herman Zaccarelli, C.S.C. *Training Managers to Train*.

Jude-York, Deborah, Ph.D., Lauren Davis, M.S., and Susan Wise, M.A. *Virtual Teaming*.

Minor, Marianne. *Coaching for Development*.

Pokras, Sandy. *Rapid Team Deployment*.

Pokras, Sandy. *Team Problem Solving, Revised Edition*.

Pokras, Sandy. *Working in Teams*.

Simons, George. *Working Together*.

Wingfield, Barb and Janice Berry. *Retaining Your Employees*.

Other Related Reading:

Cook, Marshall. *Effective Coaching*. NY: McGraw-Hill, 1999.

Maxwell, John. *The 17 Indisputable Laws of Teamwork*. Nashville, TN: Thomas Nelson Publishers, 2001.